Keep an eye out for QR codes!

Scan them with a phone, it will bring the pages to life in animated videos and more!

For Ben.

It is OK to feel.

Mamá.

Written by: Sharon Chan
Illustrated by: Daniela Rojas Arias

This is the story of a dragon named Purple.

His eyes were purple,
lavender purple.

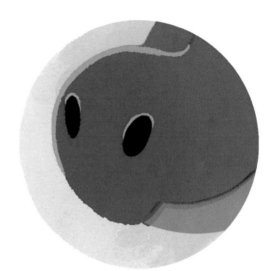

His nose was purple,
eggplant purple.

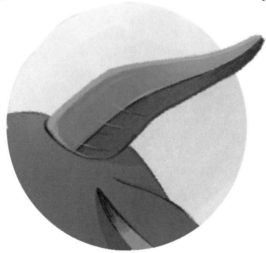

His horns were purple,
periwinkle purple.

His chest and belly were purple,
iris purple.

His body was purple,
mulberry purple.

His wings and tail were purple,
raisin purple.

Purple was the kindest and noblest dragon of all.

The most purple of Purple was his heart.

The purpleness of his heart showed whenever he was around.

The love his friends had for Purple was profound.

He helped the grandpa dragon by shovelling the snow off his walk when he hurt his back.

He helped the little dragon
by making him chicken soup
when he got croup.

Purple was a friend you
could always count on.

Then one day, Purple didn't seem purple at all.
He was as blue as blue can be.

Why was Purple now blue?
Was he hungry or tired?
What happened that turned him blue?

Purple felt sad, you see.

So, he sat in his front yard under a big tree with a big glass of iced tea.

He helped the mommy dragon by bringing her lunch when she brought home her newborn son.

The mommy dragon passed by, as he began to drink his tea.

She said:

"It's so nice to see you, Purple, my friend."

She then smiled and waved.

Purple's blue began to fade.
Then, grandpa dragon knocked on Purple's gate.

He said:

"Purple, I baked you a cake to say thanks for
all you do for me every day."

Purple turned a
little bit less blue.

Finally, not sick anymore, the little dragon came to Purple's front yard. He sat beside Purple. He didn't say a thing, just kept him company.

Purple suddenly turned purple again.

Purple smiled and said:

"Sometimes, all we need is a smile and a wave. Or a treat baked with love. Or to sit in silence with someone when having a bad day."

"All I needed today was my friends. They helped me turn purple again, at my own pace, without rush or haste."

"Especially you, little dragon. You sat silently with me, in the bluest of blue days."

Purple, The Dragon, focuses on emotional understanding and acceptance through empathy.

We all have felt intense emotions that sometimes we cannot control, and sometimes we don't even know how to control them. The idea of Purple's story is to deliver a message of acceptance of our own emotions. We believe that by accepting that it is okay to feel what we feel, we will be able to cope and manage our emotions better.

For everyone who needs to accept their emotions, it is OK to feel.

Made in the USA
Las Vegas, NV
12 March 2025

19458003R00021